Prayers
like
SHOES

Published by
•
Whit Press
4701 SW Admiral Way, #125
Seattle, WA 98116
•
PO Box 13275 / mail
252 E Pearl / ship
Jackson WY 83002
•
www.whitpress.org
•
ISBN 978-0-9720205-8-9
Library of Congress Control Number:
2008938363

 Whit Press books are made possible in major part by the generous
support of Nancy Nordhoff, Kate Nelson, Margot Snowdon,
Sherri Ontjes, our individual contributors and the following
organizations:

• The Seattle Foundation
• Seattle Office of Arts & Cultural Affairs
• The Breneman-Jaech Foundation
• Hill-Snowdon Foundation
• The Glaser Foundation

For you all, our most heartfelt thanks and gratitude.

Hedgebrook Writer's Series

Hedgebrook is a retreat for women writers on Whidbey Island in Washington State. At Hedgebrook we believe in the power of radical hospitality—if you feed and nurture a writer's body, mind and spirit, and provide a quiet place where she can settle into the stillness of her soul—she will write to the core of her truth.

A day of writing at Hedgebrook ends in the farmhouse kitchen—where writers share a meal, their writing, their stories and the breakthroughs and roadblocks in their writing process. Over 1000 women have come to Hedgebrook since our founding in 1988, from across the U.S. and as far away as Zimbabwe, Thailand, Saudi Arabia and India.

Whit Press believes that assuring a place for women poets and storytellers to publish their work is an act of hope in action. It is grounded in the certainty that the written word transcends barriers of culture, race, and class, and intimately connects us to one another's lives—as individuals, as communities, and as a planet.

Both Whit Press and Hedgebrook are committed to connecting women writers with audiences worldwide. This annual book series is a physical manifestation of that vision.

Welcome to the second edition of the Hedgebrook Writer's Series!

for Peace

Prayers
like
SHOES

Ruth Forman

Whit
Press

Seattle, Washington • Jackson Hole, Wyoming • www.whitpress.org

The Sun's One Good Eye

the sun's one good eye

is on/ you/ rise up n shine

like you sposed to

Prayers Like Shoes

Prayers Like Shoes   12
Daughter and Sky   14
Mama   15
Not a Delicate Daughter   16
Perhaps You're a Song   17
Sisters   18
What the Storefront Window Said   19
These   20
What's a Woman Without Good Stories   21
Layin On Hands Woman   22
If I Forget to Dance   24

Love Note

These Hips   26
What the Stove Said   27
He Don't Know   28
Forgive me   29
Step   30
Play With Your Own Self   31
Classified #7   32
This Morning   33
Let Down All Your Doors   34
Aphrodite   35
He Told Me   36
Man   38
Give Me All Your Worries   40
Come   41
Love Note   42
Finish Me   43
Equestrian   44
Tailor   45
Sari   46
Night's Piercing   47

Stand

The Water   50
The Usual Suspects   51
Axis of Evil   52
The Air Above Our Tongues   53
Perhaps   54
Believe   55
Poem Before Mangos Beans n Rice   56
Newscaster   58
When We Were Not Looking   60
Bike   61
Son   62
Jenin, Palestine on this 10th Day of April   63
Who   64
Six   65
She's Not Afraid Today   66
At Ramadan 2002   67
Stand   70

May Peace Come

Wish   72
Prayer for New Orleans   73
Surrender   74
Koi   75
After Death   76
You Keep Me from Burying My Heart   77
Deliverance   78
Lazarus   79
Beloved   80
Violin   81
After the War   82
I Sing Myself Into a Pearl   83
Even You   84
You a Star in Drag   85
Untitled   86
Becoming   87
May Peace Come   88

Acknowledgements   92
About the Author   93
Colophone   94
About Whit Press   95

Prayers Like Shoes

Prayers Like Shoes

I wear prayers like shoes

pull em on quiet each morning
take me through the uncertain day

don't know
what might knock me off course

sit up in bed
pull on the right
then the left
before shower before teeth

my mama's gift
to walk me through this life

she wore strong ones
the kind steady your ankles
i know
cause when her man left/ her children
gone/ her eldest son without goodbye
they the only ones keep her
standing

i saw her
still standing

mama passed on
some things to me
ma smile sense a discipline
ma
subtle behind

but best she passed on
girl you go to God
and get you some good shoes
cause this life ain't steady ground

now i don't wear hers
you take em with you you know
but i suspect they made by the same company
pull em on each morning
first the right   then the left

best piece a dress
i got

Daughter and Sky

Mama swept today
white boomerangs cross
a christian blue sky
blue
just her color dress

wind as i speak
ease
them clouds into wisps
no worry
knowing her
she sweep em again tomorrow
she in heaven
but she like a clean floor

Mama

every so often i think of you
call your name and imagine
you answer

not a voice
but a thought
so quiet i do not know
is it you
or me

does not matter

do it
more and more think
less and less
i am crazy

only closer to the invisible

is it loss
that teaches
such beautiful intangible things

Not a Delicate Daughter

nor will i be
a delicate wife i suppose
look at the thick a my legs

sometimes i wish i made a delicate woman
the kind men dip on a dance floor
whirl in hello
hover cross a threshold

wonder will he lift me
or will i just hold his hand
and we step together

wonder if delicate women
ever wish they were me
solid. hard to move

i wonder do we all
wish something else
for something
already
perfect

Perhaps You're a Song

Perhaps you're a song
waiting to be whistled tween some man's lips
perhaps you're a prayer
folded tween his hands
perhaps you're a love poem
waiting to be written

or
perhaps you're already written
n wait
for someone
to decipher your language

or perhaps you're not waiting
not waiting for anyone at all

perhaps you're already all a these things
a song a whistle a prayer a poem
playing
just for the beauty
of itself

Sisters

let down yr shoes

walk the ground

concrete

sand

or stone

red clay

field

or street

walk the ground

n know
what it is to be a woman

solid

                  alone

beautiful.

What the Storefront Window Said

When you catch your reflection
may you
stumble

on
pure
joy

These

These breasts
fulla stories
of lips n teeth n hands

sigh to ma feet

somebody take these stories please

we jus wanna bud young again n

free   chase fireflies in tall tall grass

still
they mature
a little softer
a little sad
but I swear they dare a grace
in how they round n sway
in underwire

all I wished em not to be
in a bedroom mirror at 13
big wide fulla themselves
they did not listen

n I am so glad

they musta known
I would need all this woman
to travel wit

What's a Woman Without Good Stories

travelin inside her travelin round her
what's a woman without good stories feeding her
like mashed potatoes n vinegar greens
fingers n a good mouth at midnight

what's a woman without good stories i ask you

i know a woman go looking for things to feed her
looking in places leave her empty
empty n not knowing why

a woman got ta have good stories
in the kitchen in the street
in the bedroom in the wind

stories make her know which step a good step
how to keep a back straight
n why it's a good idea to keep singing
even when yr purse feel light

Layin On Hands Woman

for V. Kali

Somebody need to write about a baptism

how a layin on hands by a holy sister open all 7 chakras
n rinse out unholiness in one touch
how angels sing through her palms on your back
when she ask how you doin
"how you doin"
sometimes you want to cry
her palms on your back and yes they hold on

til you answer
all your stories
even if you don't want to say
she look in your eyes and read anyway
pull out that stuff don't belong

your bones fall away
leaving only spirit like
water under Moses' hand
for your own real self to pass

n don't let her be wearin red
Lord don't let her be wearin red
you wonder/ when she let go
can you still stand
but yes
you have bones
and yes you fortified
and yes you one a God's children
cuz he just held you and breathed into ya heart
and yes you be taller
and yes you be clean
and no you can't stop that smile on your face

and yes you be family
and yes you belong
and yes you holy once again

n I don't know who she is really
this layin on hands woman
some Ojibwe chief with a corn pipe come back to the buffalo children
Harriet come to lead us to ourselves
God come remind us he love to rock the salt n pepper dreads

all I know
eucalyptus lavender woman
we exit your touch
we someone sweet angel chile
baptized
by our own inside rain.

If I Forget to Dance

If i forget to dance
remind me

yes if i forget to dance
take my hand
lead me to the polished floor
help me take off my shoes
put on myself

Love Note

These Hips

these hips ripe plums
don't believe
come
taste

these midnight moons
made a sugar's juice
know how to curve a line
make a knife shiver
in anticipation

these hips ripe plums
don't believe
run yr hand long this

n tell me

God did not know what She was doing
when She
gentled her hand
in a half moon
two times
smoothed
the most perfect
fruit
on earth

What the Stove Said

Need me some ambidextrous love
sweet and salty at the same time
someone love me both handed
day and night

need me some ambidextrous love
touch me on the inside n the out
love me on the bottom n the top
reach me to heaven burn me up

need me some love right here
and some left me hummin
into my 9 o'clock

now you know that's got to be
some good stuff

looking to find me two good hands
from one good god almighty
hope he get here soon
cause I sure nough
got something
for him to cook

He Don't Know

He don't know how he make me pat my do
He don't know how he make me dream a hands
He don't know how he make me knock my hips
Make this woman to think so
And feel I don't got a momma

Forgive me

i was mistaken

opened and opened you
in my palms
thinking i held love

offered
my legs my lips sweet
nutmeg stomach
to run your hands
n remember
innocence n skin

but when dawn stole night's pages
found myself alone
no hands but mine no body but mine
no face but mine frowning the light

thought i held a seed budding love
but it was a peach pit hard as stone
you slipped into my heart, magician
when i wasn't looking
growing itself already into something
i don't understand

my heart feels not the same

forgive me
when i reached for your hand
thought i grasped love

i was mistaken.

Step

get off me man
stop worryin me
stop sniffin up ma drawers n
grinnin in ma face
climbin in ma mouth twistin words inside out
oh what you sayin is…

get off me man
get
yr hands off ma ass
yr eyes out ma back
yr mouth out ma ears
talkin crooked call it straight

brush off me man
brush off step back step off jump   back
i said get off
here

leave me to walk this street in peace
I got places to go
n you
fuckin wit ma step.

Play With Your Own Self

A woman's happiness does not depend on you. Depends on her and her alone. Do not try to mold her like silly putty, imprint your cartoons of love. Stretch her to a string of patience trying to take her apart. Throw her to the floor to see if she bounces toss her to a friend to catch. Do not cut her with stencils knives or cookie cutters. Knead blue or green into her skin. Not your play dough, not your silly putty, not the field for all your games. She clay mixed with the dust of the Old One and waters of Yemaja. Holds footprints of the ancestors and seeds of those to come. If you forget ancient soil you forget your own self and where you come from. Get over yourself. She is not a game. If you must play, play with your own self.

Classified #7

who will gather
the shards of my heart
hold them with two warm palms

my hands don't reach
these arms too long

i stand
in pieces
the world winds
around
sometimes slow sometimes fast
sometimes slow
sometimes
i walk praying
the rattle of this heart not so loud
for people to hear

sit
in a block of sun listening
for warmth on my skin
worst times can't get out of bed
for fear this heart cracks even more

tried tape and glue
even Divine thread from God's lovers
but i fear
i need two hands
to make a home inside my center
keep pieces of this heart together
like two palms in prayer.

This Morning

the wind whispers my ear
do not go outside
it is so much nicer
inside your heart

Let Down All Your Doors

I am coming in
to love you

Aphrodite

heart open as the sea
arms wide as horizon
come find me
at the edge of yr shore

He Told Me

he an upright bass
singing
under a silver lining sky for me gently
he descended into my smile elegant as dusk told me
sidewalk style   cool heat looking dangerous in denim he sweet
like Louisiana barbeque smothered in smokehouse blues

if only i would taste

saw my heart glow to an ember

see red i be all blues
n blues not just g-minor
blues got high n beautiful n everything in between
fingers strumming cross
your chords let you know good when you feel
good let you know bad when you feel bad n
ain't that the best a life
telling you the truth he said
i be a silhouette
carved from the bark of our people n the dawn
of our dreams
n when we join hands
leave your worries
hummin to no one like a lonely fm dial
I be
an indigo touch
calling your name

now sophistication more than a word
        it's the way you stroll a tune in
someone's head   color their moment   fragrance their thought

let me into your life

he said this
in the smooth stutter of Monk on keys i could not help myself
this smoky bass man
could not help myself
i saw us in a get back glide together
saw us under a swaggering skyline
in the scat and answer of a 2 am jazz groove
his pulse/ my music or was it my pulse/ his music
a bebop on the round side a life

i be all blues   he said

what could i do
but believe him

Man

You a storm coming or a breeze
you steel you suede you subtle
a two-tone hustle

whose prints you wear on your being
hands you come from
who knows your stories
who cares about each one

ask cause I want to know
the color hovering beneath your wings
is it silver   sapphire   gold

where you dream of going
when you look out your morning window
who put that dream there

who was your father
who was your teacher
how much did it matter
did you ever let them know

n your path
a line straight
or curving at those inopportune places
your scars
where you hide them

your stroll
where it come from
what genius you carry in your sleeve
what you wear around your neck
does it choke or set you free

ask cause I want to know
what life knits into your fabric

and in thirty-three years
what will we say about you
faded photograph pewter frame
will we say
they don't make them like that
anymore

Give Me All Your Worries

I like to see you travel light

Come

My eyes need
something easy
come rest yourself
by here

Love Note

Open me like a letter
read me
word by word

answer

fold me in your envelope
seal me with your tongue
and send me

Finish Me

with your kiss
just finish me
gone.

Equestrian

So nice
when you reach inside
the wild horse in me
braid my mane
whisper my ear
you don't have to ride
just watch me run
in all my beauty

is it any wonder
i always come back from the woods
to feel your hands
brush me down
piece by
piece

Tailor

You have made me silk

I do not fight anymore
lay in your lap
my head
a moment of peace
this breath
mine yours slow
holding
time
between us

your fingers
gentle tailor
sew me
between these days
over
under your heart
between
your endless longing
my rough edges fold
smooth
under your slow palm
I do not crunch or crackle
you've spun me
when I wasn't looking
tailor

you have made me silk

Sari

And if I was a length of silk
I would run through your hands
like a gleaming sari
turn slightly for you in the light
sometimes gold
sometimes amber
sometimes the flame of a tiger lily
wrap myself around your waist
remind you fine things
love
to be loved

Night's Piercing

A tiny diamond winks
the burnt blue sky

night's nose piercing

she sports it
to remind you
despite your city's sequins
she still knows
how to knock
you off
your heart

Stand

The Water

holds nothing but everything
the body made of
and if we destroy the water
what makes us think
we are not next

The Usual Suspects

*"The greatest trick the Devil ever pulled
was convincing the world he didn't exist."*
—Verbal, in *The Usual Suspects*

if the greatest trick the devil ever pulled
was to convince the world he didn't exist
the greatest trick of a military government:
   convince the world to stand behind
as it aims for peace

Axis of Evil

My 13 inch Sony spits words
terror   horror   weapons of mass destruction
I hold up a mirror to my television
but it has no eyes
and reception goes only one way
into my living room

The Air Above Our Tongues

We do not speak. afraid
of what might happen to us

the air above our tongues
prays for us to speak. afraid
of what might happen
if we don't

Perhaps

you might want to shoot the sun also
since
she is not cooperating with you
today

Believe

I don't believe in now
I believe in soon
I believe in then
but they won't tell me
all what happened
I believe in me
when I look from in to out
I believe in you I believe in us
we believe in ourselves
again and again
no matter how bad now is
I guess this makes us human
maybe I believe in now
if now not what they tell me but what I know
yes what I know and I do know
I do know
a lot

Poem Before Mangos Beans n Rice
July 16, 2001

Somebody take these tears
before I cook them tonight
got two mouths to feed
black beans rice and mango salsa

take this anger
I don't want it in their food
to churn their stomachs
something not right they will say
something not right

NPR tells me
the suicide bomber claimed by Islamic jihad
kills two women/ injures others
at a bus stop
blows himself up in the process
in retaliation
two tanks open fire at a Palestinian checkpoint

and how many people die I ask the radio
they do not tell me
move on to the next story

again five minutes later
NPR tells me about the suicide bomber
the slain two women and the Palestinian government
denounces this action/ to retaliate
Israeli tanks
storm and open fire a Palestinian checkpoint

again I listen
how many killed?
the radio tells me
about farmers in Idaho

the silence not right

the missing part of the story
my hands want to pull out of the radio
and it's not there
no one will tell me
how many Palestine children and women and men they kill

and I know this half story posing as a full story
I am a Black woman in America
and when you Black in America
everything suspect

I am a woman cooking dinner
this evening black beans rice and mango salsa
I will not cook anger into it
for two mouths of people I love
cook it into this poem instead
poetry she got an iron stomach

but I wonder about people at the Palestine border
how many have iron in their stomachs
how many die
who like me tries to cook dinner?
what does she have to cook?
where does she
put her tears
so they don't enter the bellies of people she loves

Newscaster

do you sleep well at night
do you swallow your words or just
spit them at us

do you feel shame at the puppetry
makes your mouth move to   how much is it they pay you?

you say with a smile
"Find out if there'll be a showdown in Iraq"
as if this entertainment
as if it means nothing
with another bite of a hungry man's dinner

meanwhile
who packs their last belongings
wondering what should stay what should go
who hurries across a border she's never seen
to avoid becoming bone

who draws your strings

do you choke sometimes at the movement of your jaw
really I want to know

11pm Tuesday night Los Angeles

you the willing smoke of the Wizard of Oz
and I must admit
we all scared
but like Dorothy
I want to peek behind the curtain

do they pay you enough
to not feel your own words
or do you really believe them

do you sleep at night
if so
what do you dream
and in your dreams
do you get to say
what you really want to say

When We Were Not Looking

This war take a toll on you
hear it in your laugh
thinner than it used to be
still hug me in your voice though
and i hug back
my hug thinner than it used to be
this war take a toll on me too
no measure really
guess we could count our number of breaths
measure the way our eyes look at strangers
how many new jeans we buy
but how do you measure such things
how do you replace what left us
when we were not looking

Bike

The sky's a beautiful breath blue and you ride your bike with family in a wide place across the red dirt. Sunday and the bike rides pretty good, you ahead of everybody. And you look up again and things in the sky now. Falling in clusters they come towards you explosions and planes skidding away. You hear the sound and shakes of the ground splitting somewhere far behind you and did I say you are a child on this bike and does this bike ride fast enough on the dirt you think and get off the bike and run, but still hold on to the handlebars. And now smaller things coming down metal to go into your body and you don't know where everyone is and a man face down in the dirt and do you stop or keep going. Keep going. Surely one of these metal things is going to meet you and the bombs all around now you want to dodge them, which way to go? Fate. Surely you will die and it's okay really. You liked your bike and riding but which way to hide. Some rocks you get behind see others do the same in this moment this magical moment of a blue breath sky falling alien things that shake the whole world. Who has a camera to see this? Seven people and a man back there somewhere in the dirt. The bombs they somehow missed most of you. The sky turns rose and magenta music it seems the whole sky plays a rose music loud to remind you you still alive. They may come again, but you are still alive. You hurry away your bike hold tight to the handlebars.

Son

Don't trouble his body
with your bullets
he stands tall for eight years old

Perhaps your sniper rifle
aims at 250 worms crawling his scalp
with no clean water

Perhaps your tank
targets his betraying stomach
full of breath

Congo Sri Lanka Sudan Afghanistan does it matter

Perhaps your eye
aims his future
yes maybe who he will become frightens you

As it should

Jenin, Palestine on this 10th Day of April

What would your grandfather say of your bullets
what would he say of your M-16
does he know where you got it
does he wonder where you got
the red in your eyes   and the blood
what does he think of the blood
on the wall of that home
and what does he think of the blood
in the street
letters D – O – G
you scrawl on that man's forehead
before you line him up for heaven

does it remind him of things
do you remind him of things

Who

In war

who good who evil who innocent

who exact terror whose ashes right

worthy to cry for

Six

every six seconds a woman raped
where your weapons now?

six more seconds and a woman raped
or did you forget already

name me then in your anger name
me then in your protection name
me.

She's Not Afraid Today

to say she's afraid
more than yesterday

this blossoming napalm she tried to stop
not that her voice so big
but it marched with so many
and now the voices muffle
like plastic soldiers
in the khaki pocket of a boy child

she doesn't have her words today
someone put them in a pocket
make sure no one could hear
but they have teeth these words
know how to use them
this very moment
they work their way
to the open air

At Ramadan 2002

A forehead kisses this blessed earth
calls Allah for Mercy and Guidance
and Mercy

the air has changed
the whole world cries

I understand prayer
I understand an FBI office does not grace
a place of prayer

we
Black people
have had FBI shoot down our greatest leaders
tap our phones/ blue eyes behind binoculars watch us bathe our children
hurl exploding packages into our churches and living rooms
this a violent country with no memory
people on the sidewalk look at us
as if we the enemy

this country got a sickness
you been bit
I see your eyes turning, turning
doesn't anyone see? we just people living our lives
they crush us with their steel boots/ my bones crack
and they call us violence

beware
here the glass shine
but the perspective it lends inversely twisted
here those coinless get punished/ and those with coins receive everything free
the sick cannot get health insurance/ the healthy as many doctor visits as they'd like
and everyone is free/ so long as they shop

I see them in airports treat you like they treat us
understand your fury but not without irony
15 years ago
a young Persian man could not believe police pulled 16 year olds out of cars
to make snow angels on the Los Angeles concrete cause they 16 and Black
wonder what he think now

imbalance happens to all of us in the middle of grave injustice
we juggle our minds
each one
trying to figure out how to survive this air
some of us numb
some shrivel
some of us eat each other
some explode

but I believe
imbalance we right by changing the air around us
with our walk
our voice
out loud

for me this means
putting these words into the air
a small gesture really but all I can do
to let you know I understand

yes. people die on top of each other while your neighbors shop the Beverly Center
trying on the latest lipstick. their biggest dilemma
Viva Glam or Lancôme
and yes. Kissinger worms his hand back into U.S. military grip
and yes. people do not know bills and clauses pass
to steal fathers away from their families in the middle of the night and
look into each and every living room and computer and
tap each and every phone/ to protect
monopolies as they continue to suck
all resources from this earth and two legged creatures
and this is not the half of it
and this is too much to fathom and drink mint tea

but bring up your beautiful smile
name justice
with your walk
your voice
out loud
there are these small moments happening across the city
there really are
and across the country
there really are
that collectively change this air of fear

transform the very air in which you move
let it announce love. justice. here
remind someone something.

Stand

why so afraid to stand up?
someone will tell you
sit down?

but here is the truth
someone will always tell you
sit down

the ones we remember
kept standing

May Peace Come

Wish

you
a house of bright windows
and no fear of rocks

Prayer for New Orleans

Sleep now darlin rest yourself
new day comin
new day comin

sleep now darlin rise in the morning
death gone now
death gone now

took his numbers
left you wandrin
sleep now darlin rest yourself

truth come soon now
truth will out
truth come soon now
truth soon out

angels see you
travel with you
not alone now
not alone now

new day comin
new day dawnin
rest yourself love rest yourself

Surrender

I would gladly lay down all my weapons
to rest my soul
on your shoulder

Koi

for Christine

have you seen a woman collapse have you
seen her bones melt while she grasps
a glass of white wine remembering have you
forced yourself not to look away

not easy
to hold up a grieving woman she falls through your fingers
like ashes of a husband passed seven weeks ago

have you felt tears weave the air from her fine piano have you
felt yourself crack

you still dare walk these halls
this oak floor bare foot

what gives you the right to open the refrigerator
find enough for a salad among celery going bad you

climb into her bed empty though you in it who are you

to uphold this house struggling death and life who are you

to hold her on your right shoulder pat her
into shape prayers and song for leavening

tell her she does good kiss her cheek when she lets you
touch her head when she's not busy
outrunning her heart, garden hose and laundry basket

maybe it's enough to bear witness with ivory candles
to a woman risen and fallen by love

still enough magic in her right hand to chase life
into a gold Koi you find gasping

on the ground she places him in water
coaxes his body
clockwise til he swims

with all fins

After Death

Sometimes we wonder what the world would be without our father. our mother. our partner. and then we find out. as if a giant story rolled itself up and threw itself away. a story we lived in. gone.

and then it is just you.

and then the world changes before your eyes, sharper, blurrier. as if you could put your fingers through and get to the other side. whatever that holds. it be that way sometimes. the ones we love cross over and the bridge lingers.

but then we look at the people around us. the ones with their hands on our sleeves, holding on. sometimes it's only the hands on your elbows you feel. sometimes it's enough. sometimes it's everything.

here's to the blessings around you. the hands on your arms gently tugging you back into the space where people love you. hold you dear to them. the blessing that such people exist. the blessing that you had a part in making them feel this way.

and then you know there is a tradition. just as you love the person that has crossed beyond the veil, these people love you. and that person must have taught you something right. and oh how they smile to see you comforted.

forgive my presumption in talking about these things. i don't know you well. but fragile times call for a bit of courage. piece by piece.

You Keep Me from Burying My Heart

message from V. Kali

A year ago today I buried my daughter
but I did not
bury my heart

thought about *bury my heart at wounded knee*
and I said I need to call
those who come to mind
because you all keep me
you keep me
you continue to keep me

so I want to thank you
for keeping my heart
above the ground
oh

keeping me above ground .

nothing wrong with laying on the ground
but
once you go below
hard to rise up
and raise up
and all that Lazarus vibration

Sometimes I wonder how I keep from going under

now I know

you keep me, huh
you keep me

a year ago today I buried my daughter

Deliverance

Passover, 2008

The hand of God is with us
the palm of the greatest one
lifts us

when we forget
let us remember
and when we remember
return

to our promise
our land of birth and right
and deliverance

the hand of God is with us
the breath of the greatest one in us

let us speak
remember our praise
pray
remember our name

return
to our promise
our land of deliverance

replete with light and angels
calling

calling
for our song

Lazarus

i, lazurus
these last seven years
but now time to rise
reaching
for the great hand
holds us all
take me up
from this death
swing back the rock
let me look into my new Beloved's eyes
and rise

Beloved

be my mouth/ how I speak
be my ears/ what I hear
be my mind be my thought
be my peace

be my eyes/ how I see
be my back/ how I stand
be my heart be my heart
how I heal me

be my hand/ how I touch
be my legs/ pace my feet
be my breath be my peace
how I go

Violin

i was a fine violin
til i broke in half
could not take the pressure
n split

now i sit
gluing myself with prayer
and gentle song

each day a little here a little here
calling on the master musician
to touch
where i can't reach

he places his hand in the small
of my spine

my seams fuse together
perhaps more beautiful than before
perhaps more fine

perhaps these cracks
others follow with their fingers like a map
ahhh, I know that place
see how she came together
here n here

i was complete once

now
completing
gluing myself with prayer
and gentle song

and in my ears the music
of the master

After the War

you who welcome me both arms
i have missed your touch
i have missed your breath in mine

I Sing Myself Into a Pearl

I sing myself into a pearl
roll into the open mouth of the Divine
fear kept me tight as an oyster's shell
but with life prying me open with its cruel and beautiful blade
and the itch of love within my heart
my pieces gather themselves
as sand and sand gathering hands and
with a sigh
sing
into a pearl
giving up all difference
for a globe
perfect as this earth
bright as the source of love itself
smooth as breath
and so
when the Divine swallows me
i go down easy
like an eager lover
after nights and nights
of separation
willing to sacrifice everything
for the sweet oblivion
of union

Even You

Be a chalice
a channel a flow
a river an outlet a sea
be a tunnel a course a lotus a song
a journey a road a traveling word
open your hands your eyes your mouth
your very being
let the universe roar through you
not embarrassed
to be beautiful in an ugly place
beauty changes everything
to its rightful state of being

even you.

You a Star in Drag

got clothing n skin to fool us all
even adopted a new language
and take to walking on two feet

but your eyes give it away
twinkle and shine despite themselves
despite you
trying to blend in
to your sidewalk
when I look in them I'm a place
I know
somewhere in my DNA

someplace like night sky
when all is peace   no more than zero wars in any given country
when a mother puts up her feet after a good fried chicken dinner
and a loved one washes the plates
when the sea whispers that secret song
only the moon listening

all this I see in your eyes
despite your trying to look unimpressed
by these words I say
but it's too late
I cannot be fooled   my heart
has made its decision

you a star
in drag

Untitled

The spirit lights on us
oh how lucky the world
if we are ready

Becoming

She's a girl
a woman
girl in a woman   never left
that girl
this woman
left other things
that hand round her throat
that sweet grip
kept her from singing
becoming a new woman
not sure when she'll get there
but these steps feel good
like bare feet on grass
sure as her grandmother's dress
sweet as her unborn humming
a language she understands just fine
she stops looking
in mirrors for answers
steps inside herself instead
this place feels like a garden
this lawn she tends with diligence
she combs her hair with sky
braids it with rosewater
births a new moon
over redwood and evergreen
names this earth
a new name
and it includes her letters
no longer outside looking in
wondering how to make this place
stop spinning
she grabs this world
with her two hands
tilts it right
sees herself
in still water
finds
herself
becoming

May Peace Come

with each breath
each step upon the ground
each blink
may peace be called
each hand holding a hand
each blow across a face
may peace be called

each child running into his father's arms
each black baton across a brown back
each steel toe across a head
each forefinger pointing
a trigger
each falling body never to raise up
each mouth that will not close
each child calling a parent that will never come
each broken heart
may peace be called
each Bible clutched each Torah each Koran each holy book in every land
eye water spilled in pain
each blossoming belly despite us all
each you
each me reaching
to be better
for our own self
each teenager
learning her path head up back straight
each broken hand
each missing body part
each loved one looking
each safe safe bed
each sleep each wake
each new despair
each determination
each lapis night each amber morning
may peace be called

may peace be called for you my friend
may peace be called for you
may peace be called at one time
for all of us
and if by some moment
some slim chance
peace wakes
rubs her eyes to see who's calling
may she take one look
and fall in love
with us all

Acknowledgements

Grateful acknowledgement is made to the following publications, in which earlier versions of some of these poems originally appeared: *Velocity: The Best of Apples and Snakes* and *Voices from Leimert Park: A Poetry Anthology*. Earlier versions of "Prayers Like Shoes" and "You a Star in Drag" aired on **National Public Radio**. "Prayers Like Shoes" also appeared as a collaboration with Tara Ellis on *Arise*, on **Crimson Group Records**. Thanks to The Durfee Foundation, Hedgebrook, and Villa Montalvo for their generous support for this work. Grateful thanks finally to all those who've made this book possible. You know who you are.

About the Author

Ruth Forman is an acclaimed writer and poet as well as a teacher with the University of Southern California and former teacher in June Jordan's Poetry for the People program at UC Berkeley. The author of three award-winning books: poetry collections *We Are the Young Magicians* and *Renaissance*, and children's book, *Young Cornrows Callin Out the Moon*, her work is widely anthologized. She provides writing workshops at schools and universities across the country and abroad, and has presented in forums such as the **United Nations**, the **National Black Arts Festival**, the PBS series *The United States of Poetry* and **National Public Radio**. Also an MFA graduate of the USC School of Cinema-Television, she frequently collaborates on music, dance, theatre, art and media projects. When not writing and teaching, she practices a passion for martial arts: classical Yang family style tai chi chuan, tai chi sword, bo staff and karate. Ms. Forman currently lives in Los Angeles.

You can learn more about her at www.ruthforman.com and www.myspace.com/ruthforman.

Colophon

The cover title type is set in Satisfaction, a font design from E-phemera font design studio. E-phemera is the creation of Andrew Leman, a Hollywood prop designer who in his quest for authenticity makes fonts as part of his work. Additional cover title and interior headline is set in Gill Sans. It was designed by Eric Gill and released by the Monotype Corporation between 1928 and 1930. Gill Sans is based on the typeface Edward Johnston, named for the innovative British letterer and teacher who designed the London Underground signage in 1916. The interior text blocks and heads were also set in Gill Sans Light.

Interior stock is Rolland Enviro 100 Trade, 55# Cream made from 100% post-consumer recycled material by the Cascades Fine Paper Group of Canada. Cover stock is 12 point coated one side only with lay flat matt film lamination.

Book design by Tracy Lamb, Laughing Lamb Design, Jackson Hole, Wyoming. Images on the cover and interior were gleaned from a variety of image banks and adapted for use by the designer.

Print production by Transcontinental Printing, G.P. of Louiseville, Quebec, Canada.

About Whit Press

SUPPORT FOR THE INDEPENDENT VOICE

Whit Press is a nonprofit publishing organization dedicated to the transformational power of the written word.

Whit Press exists as an oasis to nurture and promote the rich diversity of literary work from women writers, writers from ethnic and social minorities, young writers, and first-time authors.

We also create books that use literature as a tool in support of other nonprofit organizations working toward environmental and social justice.

We are dedicated to producing beautiful books that combine outstanding literary content with design excellence.

Whit Press brings you the best of fiction, creative nonfiction, and poetry from diverse literary voices who do not have easy access to quality publication.

We publish stories of creative discovery, cultural insight, human experience, spiritual exploration, and more.

Please visit our web site www.whitpress.org for our other titles.

Whit Press and the environment

Whit Press is a member of the Green Press Initiative. We are committed to eliminating the use of paper produced with endangered forest fiber.